Got Tape?

**Ellie
Schiedermayer**

Published by

**krause
publications**

700 East State Street • Iola, WI 54990-0001
715/445-2214 • FAX: 715/445-4087   www.krause.com

Please call or write for our free catalog of publications. Our toll-free number to place
an order or obtain a free catalog is 800-258-0929 or please use our regular business
telephone 715-445-2214 for editorial comment and further information.

Library of Congress Catalog Number 2001096289
ISBN 0-87349-426-1

Duck® brand duct tape is non-toxic; however, if you have allergies to natural rubber or latex, do not eat
or drink from any of the projects in this book.

Photos on pages 14, 34, and 42 copyrighted by The Picture People.

Dedication

This book is dedicated to my family and friends.

Acknowledgments

I would like to thank my editor, Amy Tincher-Durik, and my photographer, Bob
Best, at Krause; my mom and dad for everything; Grandma and Grandpa Grummer
and Grandma and Grandpa Schiedermayer for encouragement, supplies, and ideas; my
brothers Jon and Dan for helping with project selection; and Mike and Gail for all of
your positive input. Thanks to the models, Megan, Brittany, Don, Dan, Kris, Ross,
Sadie the dog, Laura, Daniel, and Kevin, and my friends Lauren and Anne.

Table of Contents

Belt, page 10

Bowl, page 22

Wallet, page 31

Crown, page 42

Introduction

A lot of people ask how I got into duct tape crafting. A couple of years ago, I saw a duct tape wallet and some jewelry that I thought were really cool. So, I scrounged up some tape from the basement and sat down to make my own wallet and bracelet. Then, I started experimenting with duct tape, making more things for fun—and here I am today!

My purpose in writing this book is to teach you how to make neat things out of duct tape, too. Sure, you can buy most of the items in this book at a store, but why do that when you can be unique and make them out of duct tape for practically nothing? Just look at the picture below; you can make all of the projects shown with just one roll! It's hard to believe that a material designed for the military in World War II could be used to make belts, postcards, and CD holders today—but it can!

Before you start any of the projects, it's a good idea to read Chapter 1 and try to do all of the basic techniques. Read through all directions before beginning a project to get an idea of what it requires. You may notice that the photos for some directions have red tape in them; I used this to highlight certain spots, to make them easier for you to see. Hopefully this will help you better understand the written directions. Finally, I have not given you specific instructions for decorating your projects; use the photos as a guide and try experimenting with different stickers, markers, and other embellishment tools to make them truly one-of-a-kind.

Have fun!

Ellie Schiedermayer

Just look at all of the projects you can make with one roll of duct tape!

1 General Instructions

When I'm figuring out how to make something out of duct tape, there are a few techniques I always use. These techniques form the basis of duct tape crafting, making it possible to create almost anything out of it. Here are the supplies, helpful tips, and four basic techniques you need to get rolling on duct tape projects.

Necessary Supplies

✔ Duct tape
✔ Scissors
✔ String or tape measure
✔ Ruler

Optional Supplies

✔ Colored duct tape
✔ Markers
✔ Stickers
✔ Glue gun, low temperature
✔ Any other supplies you'd like to use for decorating projects
✔ Good music

Markers and Scissors That Work Well on Duct Tape

The shiny side of duct tape is essentially plastic, making it hard to write on the surface. From my experience, permanent paint markers and Sharpies® work the best on duct tape. You can always put clear tape over the colored surface to keep words or drawings from rubbing off.

My regular scissors used to get gummed up and made working with duct tape difficult. It took some of the fun out of making projects, because I constantly had to stop and clean the gunk off of my scissors. Non-stick scissors from Fiskars® are great! They make creating with duct tape easier.

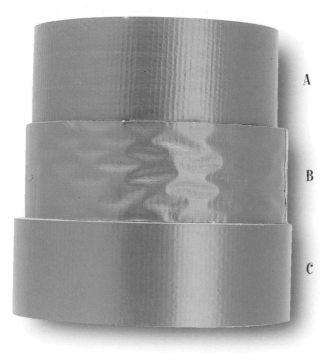

A

B

C

Choosing the Right Tape

Not all duct tape is the same! Here are some tips for choosing a good roll of traditional (gray) duct tape:

1 Observe how it looks. The roll should appear smooth and tight (like roll C). If it seems dimpled (like roll B), or if you can see texture like a string grid (like roll A), the roll might give you trouble.

2 Observe how the tape comes off of the roll. You shouldn't have to struggle to unroll it, and the top of the strip should not stretch as you pull on it.

There are many brands of duct tape currently on the market. Use the tips above to choose a good roll and experiment with what's available in your area.

Another feature available is colored duct tape. It usually comes in smaller rolls (of the same width as larger rolls) and can have a cloth or plastic texture. Colored duct tape is great for livening up your projects. Colors range from standard red, blue, black, yellow, and green to neons and even a camouflage print.

Techniques

Refer to these four techniques while you are working on the projects in Chapters 2 to 5.

Technique 1
Basic Duct Tape Sheet

This basic duct tape sheet is used in many projects in this book. The resulting crisscross pattern will give you a durable sheet.

1 Check the project you want to make for the recommended length; for example, the directions might ask you to make a duct tape sheet that is 6 inches long by three strips wide.

2 Cut a strip of duct tape to that length (6 inches) and lay it sticky side up on your work surface.

3 Roll out and cut another strip of duct tape to the same length.

4 Place the second 6-inch strip sticky side up so it slightly overlaps the edge of the first strip.

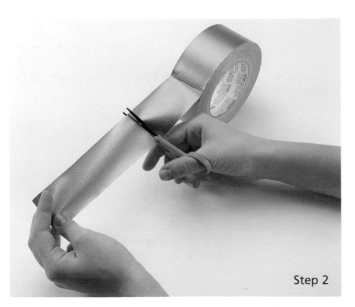

Step 2

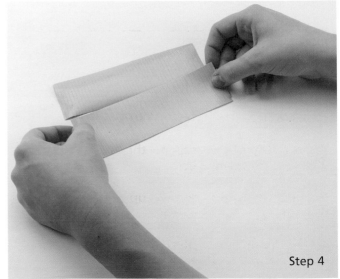

Step 4

5 Cut and overlap strips until you have the recommended number of strips for your project (in this case, three).

6 Turn the sheet so the strips are running vertically.

7 Cut a strip to lay across the sticky side up strips. Start at the top and work your way down. These

strips get placed sticky side down. Remember to overlap the edges.

8 Continue laying strips sticky side down until all of the sticky sides of the "bottom" strips are covered.

9 Trim off sticky edges.

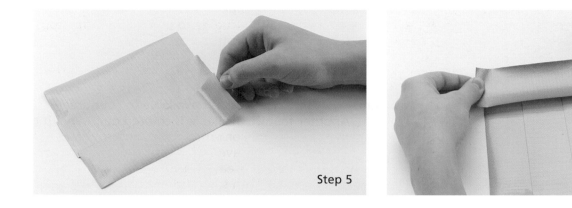

Step 5

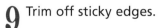

Step 7

Technique 2
Double-sided Strip

Here's a technique that can save you a lot of trouble when you only need a small two-sided strip.

1 Cut a strip of duct tape to the recommended length for the project.

2 Lay it sticky side up on your work surface.

3 Cut another strip of the same length. Place it sticky side down, directly on the first strip, matching up all edges.

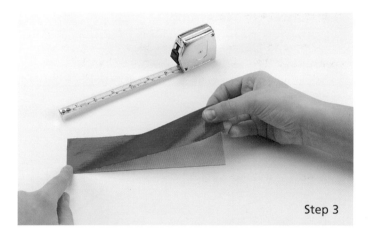

Step 3

Technique 3
Folded Strip

This is a convenient technique for making straps, bands, and other thin strips.

1 Cut a strip of duct tape to the recommended length for the project.

2 Place the strip sticky side up on your work surface.

3 Fold the strip in half the long way (so that the long edges come together).

Continued on the next page.

Here's what you get with each of the basic techniques.

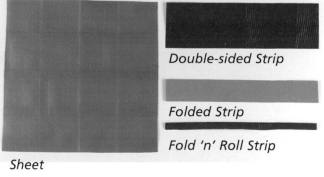

Double-sided Strip

Folded Strip

Fold 'n' Roll Strip

Sheet

4 If the strip is long and seems hard to fold, start in the center of the strip, line the two edges up, and press to make a fold.

5 Carefully press on the fold and slide fingers away from the center, keeping the edges lined up to the ends of the strip.

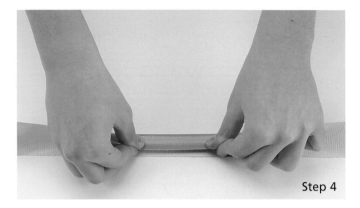

Step 4

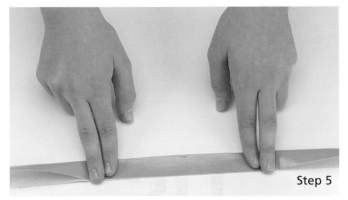

Step 5

Technique 4

Fold 'n' Roll Strip

This is a fast way to make a thin, layered strip.

1 Cut a strip of duct tape to the recommended length for the project. Place the strip sticky side up on your work surface.

2 Fold the bottom edge up 1/8 inch and press along the fold. Repeat.

3 With a rolling motion, fold your new bottom edge up 1/8 inch and again press along the fold.

4 Continue to roll to the top of the strip.

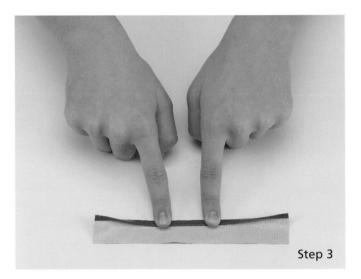

Step 3

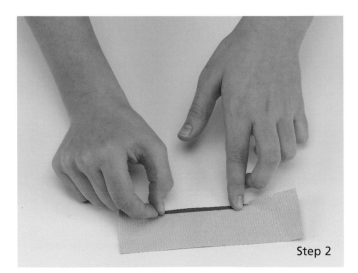

Step 2

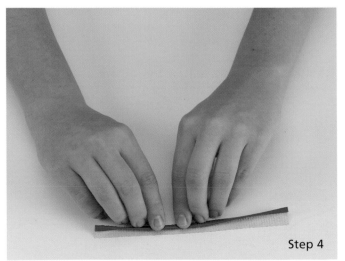

Step 4

2 Wearables

The projects in this section always seem to get the most attention because it is not often people see someone wearing duct tape!

Tie

DIFFICULTY: EASY

One day, my friend Dave forgot his tie, so I made him one out of tape and saved his neck!

You Will Need

✔ Pre-made tie*
✔ Duct tape
✔ Tape measure
✔ Scissors
✔ Scotch tape
✔ Optional: colored duct tape, stickers

* This tie will serve as your pattern. Don't worry! It will not be damaged in any way.

1 Locate the approximate center of the tie; mark with Scotch tape. **Note:** Because ties are so long, it is easier to make one half at a time.

2 Start on the skinny half of the tie. Measure from the halfway point marked in Step 1 to the tip of the tie. Make a double-sided strip this length (see page 7).

3 Cut a strip that's as long as the distance from the halfway point to the wide end.

4 Make a duct tape sheet (page 6) that is the measurement in Step 3 by two strips wide.

Continued on the next page.

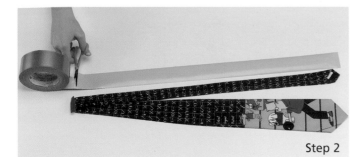

Step 2

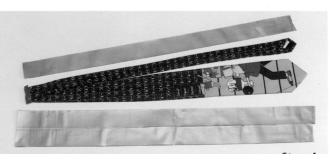

Step 4

5 Use duct tape to tape the two sections together.

6 Use Scotch tape to tape the tie onto the duct tape sheet.

7 Cut all of the way around the tie. Remove Scotch tape.

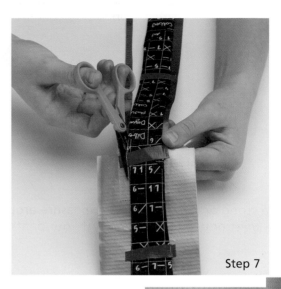
Step 7

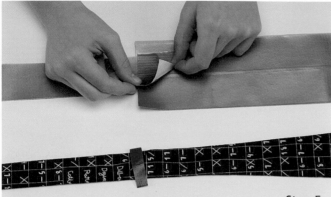
Step 5

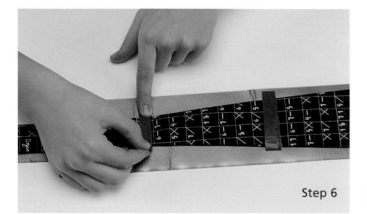
Step 6

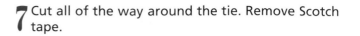

Options

Look at the back of your pre-made tie; you might find a loop there. The loop keeps the tie together when it is worn. To make a loop for your duct tape tie, make a folded strip that's 2 inches long (see page 7). Tape it onto the back of the tie with two small pieces of tape.

Belt

DIFFICULTY: INTERMEDIATE

I just didn't feel like spending $20 on a strip of leather with holes in it, so I decided to make myself a duct tape belt. I wear it at least three times a week. I hope you get lots of compliments on your duct tape belt!

You Will Need

✔ Duct tape
✔ Scissors
✔ Tape measure or string
✔ X-acto knife*
✔ Optional: colored duct tape, stickers

*For adult or supervised use only!

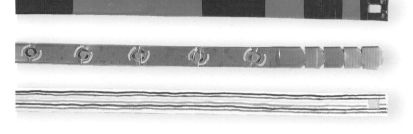

1 Use a string or tape measure to measure around your waist or wherever the top of your pants rests.

2 Add 6 inches to your waist measurement and cut a strip of duct tape to that length. Use it to make a folded strip (see page 7). Now you have your basic belt, but it needs more layers to add strength.

3 Pull out a length of duct tape from the roll but don't cut it. Take the loose end of the duct tape roll and put it on the belt diagonally at one end.

4 Wrap the roll around, pulling out tape as needed until you reach the other end of the belt.

5 Repeat Steps 3 and 4, but start the diagonal wrap in the opposite direction.

6 Cut a strip of duct tape that is the same length as the piece you cut in Step 2.

7 Lay the strip sticky side up on your work surface. Place the belt in the center of the strip.

Continued on the next page.

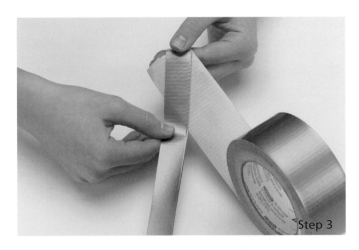

Step 3

Step 5

Step 4

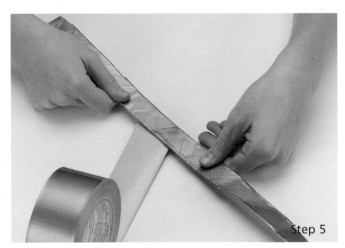

Step 5

8 Fold the top edge of the strip down and the bottom edge up onto the belt.

9 Repeat Steps 6 to 8, flipping the belt over when you center it onto the strip.

10 To make the buckle, use scissors or an X-acto knife to cut a square opening in one end of the belt. Keep it 1/4 inch from all of the sides so the opening won't break or stretch. **Note:** You can also use small strips to reinforce the buckle, wrapping them around the three thin sides of the opening.

11 On the other end of the belt, cut about eight triangles about an inch apart, as shown.

12 To fasten the buckle, take the end with the triangles, fold it in half, and put it through the square opening on the other end. Adjust to fit comfortably.

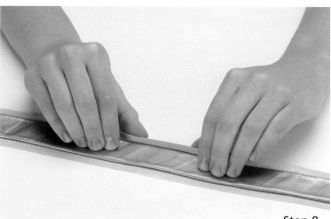
Step 8

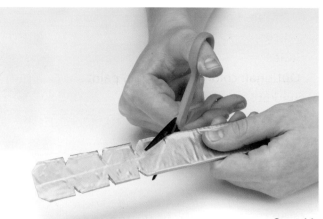
Step 11

Step 10

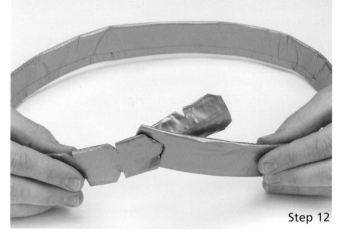
Step 12

Option
Make a reversible belt with a different design on each side!

Glasses

DIFFICULTY: INTERMEDIATE

Try leaving a pair of duct tape glasses sitting around, and you'll find people can't resist putting them on.

You Will Need

✔ Duct tape
✔ Scissors
✔ Ruler
✔ Optional: colored duct tape, paint markers

1 Make a 12-inch fold 'n' roll strip of duct tape (see page 8).

2 Cut another 12-inch strip and lay it sticky side up. Take the rolled strip from Step 1 and place it on the bottom edge of the new strip.

3 Fold and roll as before to make a double-thick strip.

4 Cut the rolled strip in half. Set the two 6-inch pieces aside (they will become the ear pieces).

5 Repeat Steps 1 to 3 using strips that are 15 inches long.

6 Cut the piece from Step 5 to the following lengths:

• Four 2-1/2-inch sections (frame top and bottom)
• Four 1-inch sections (frame sides)
• One 3/4-inch section (nose bridge)

7 To assemble, lay out frame pieces, as shown.

8 Cut eight small 1/4-inch wide strips. Connect the frame pieces (except for the nose bridge). Place tape so that it wraps around the front to the back, as shown.

9 Cut two more 1/4-inch wide strips to connect the nose bridge. The strips should start on the front of the nose bridge piece; loop around the eye frame and attach to the back of the nose bridge. Repeat for the other side.

10 Attach the ear pieces, as shown, with 1/4-inch wide strips.

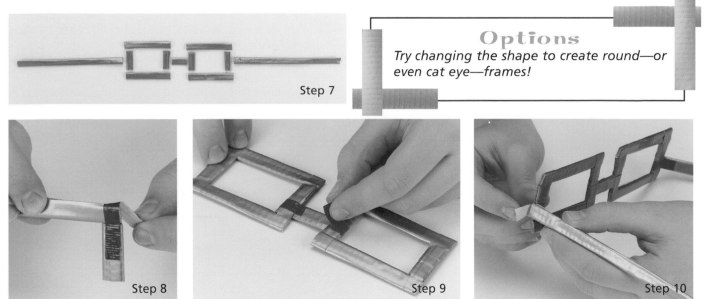

Step 7

Options
Try changing the shape to create round—or even cat eye—frames!

Step 8

Step 9

Step 10

Bracelets, Anklets, & Necklaces

DIFFICULTY: VERY EASY

Duct tape jewelry is easy for you to make, because it doesn't involve many techniques.

You Will Need

✔ Duct tape
✔ Scissors
✔ Tape measure or string
✔ Optional: stickers, paint markers, colored duct tape

Single-strand

1 Measure your wrist, neck, or ankle with a string or tape measure.

2 Cut a strip of duct tape to this measurement, plus 1 inch.

3 Make a folded strip (see page 7) with the strip cut in Step 2.

4 Cut the design of your choice (for instance, wavy, points, etc.).

5 Cut a thin strip of tape about 1/4 inch long.

6 Bring the two ends of the jewelry together. Wrap the thin strip around where the ends meet.

Double- and Triple-strand

1 Follow Steps 1 to 4 in the Single-strand style, choosing either a zigzag or curved design. Make two strands.

2 Line up the ends of each strand. Tape the ends of the strands to your work space.

3 Weave the strands together by putting one strand over, then under, the other strand.

4 Finish as described in Steps 5 and 6 of the Single-strand style.

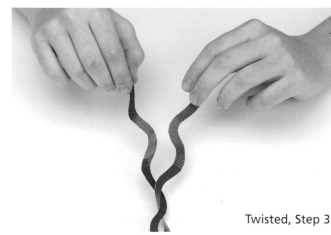

Twisted, Step 3

Twisted, Step 4

Finger or Toe Ring

DIFFICULTY: VERY EASY

One of my first encounters with duct tape was at a summer camp. Our counselor made duct tape rings for all of the girls . . . and I still have mine!

You Will Need

✔ Duct tape

✔ Scissors

✔ Tape measure or string

✔ Optional: stickers, paint markers, colored duct tape

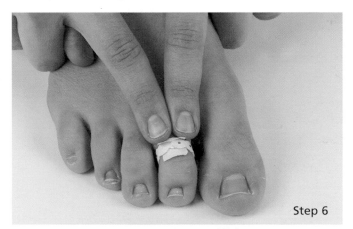

Sandal instructions can be found on page 40.

1 Measure your finger or toe with a string or tape measure.

2 Cut a piece of tape to the length of the string.

3 Make a fold 'n' roll strip with the piece cut in Step 2 (see page 8).

4 Cut a very thin strip of duct tape, about 1/8 inch long.

5 For a finger ring, pull the two ends of the folded strip together and use the thin strip to connect them.

6 For a toe ring, put the folded strip around your toe before taping it together; otherwise, you won't be able to get it on.

Step 1

Step 6

Options

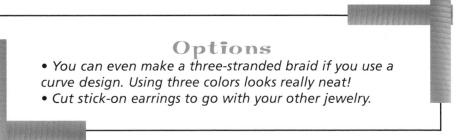

- *You can even make a three-stranded braid if you use a curve design. Using three colors looks really neat!*
- *Cut stick-on earrings to go with your other jewelry.*

Visor

***Visors are fun to wear with friends . . .
Here I am with my editor!***

You Will Need

✔ Duct tape

✔ Scissors

✔ Ruler

✔ Optional: colored duct tape, stickers, Sharpies, buttons

1 Make a duct tape sheet that is 11 inches long by five strips wide (see page 6).

2 Use the pattern to cut out the shape of the visor from the duct tape sheet.

3 Cut a strip that is about 12 inches long. Make a folded strip (see page 7). This will be the strap.

4 Tape one end of the strap to one end of the visor.

5 Put the visor on and wrap the strap around your head until it fits comfortably. Tape the strap to the other side of the visor. Cut off any extra.

Step 4

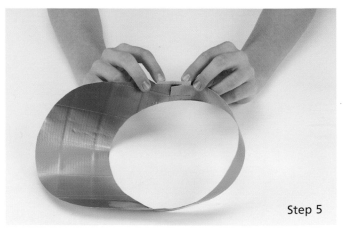

Step 5

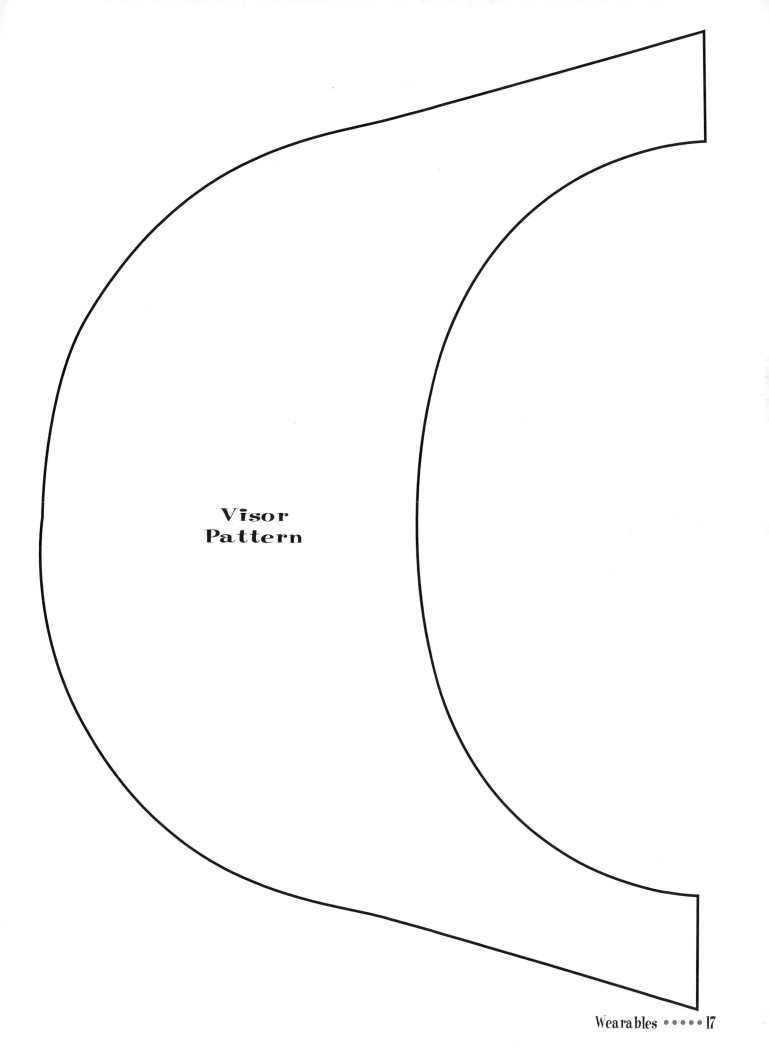

Visor
Pattern

Clothes

My first effort toward making duct tape clothes was for an English paper. We were supposed to write an essay about something we had never done before and explain to our audience how to do it. I chose to write about how I made my duct tape pants, shown at left. I never expected that paper to turn into a book!

Before trying to make clothing out of duct tape, it is a good idea to make a couple of other projects; this way you get used to working with the tape. You might even develop some of your own techniques that will make the process easier!

To give you a general idea of how to make duct tape clothing, these are the steps I followed to make the skirt seen on the cover. Use similar techniques to make your own duct tape skirt, pants, vest, or whatever.

You Will Need

✔ Duct tape
✔ Scissors
✔ Ruler
✔ Optional: colored duct tape, stickers, Sharpies, buttons

1 Select a skirt that fits you well.

2 By using seams and edges, identify sections; my skirt had two front panels, a back section, and a waistband.

3 Make a duct tape sheet big enough for each section (see page 6).

4 Use each skirt section as a pattern to make the same section out of the duct tape sheet.

5 Piece and tape the sections to form a replica of the original skirt.

Step 1

Step 4

Tips

• Do not use an article of clothing made out of stretch material or that has a drawstring as a model. Duct tape does not stretch or gather well.
• You can use a fabric pattern. Cut off all seam allowances before transferring the pattern to the duct tape sheet. Keep in mind, though, that there is no way to tell if the clothing will fit until after it is made!
• If the sections of your clothing—the ones defined by seams and edges—are too big to handle, divide into smaller sections.
• For comfort, you may want to wear a layer of "normal" clothing under the duct tape garment.
• Remember, no buttons or zippers are needed; just tape pieces together!

Stuck at Prom

In 2001, Manco Inc., the manufacturers of Duck® brand duct tape, challenged high school students across the United States to make their prom outfits out of duct tape. The couples had to submit a photo to post on the Manco website, and site visitors voted for the best outfit. The winning couple received $2,500 each for college scholarships. Here's the 2001 winning couple and some of the other entrants! You can view all of the submissions, plus find out lots more about duct tape, at www.manco.com.

The winners (above center) and four other entries. Prom photography courtesy of Manco, Inc., makers of Duck® brand duct tape.

Home Décor

Most of the home décor projects in this chapter came about for a specific purpose:
- *Coaster. I kept leaving water marks on our wood table.*
- *Place mat. That spaghetti just seems to jump right off of my plate.*
- *Picture frame. We couldn't find a frame that went well with the picture of the duct tape pants... and so on.*

Picture Frame

DIFFICULTY: INTERMEDIATE

You know how you can never find a frame for school pictures, panoramic shots, or instant Polaroids? Well, make your own! These directions will make a frame for a 4- by 6-inch picture, but you can adjust the measurements to fit any photo.

You Will Need
✔ Duct tape
✔ Scissors
✔ Ruler
✔ Picture to frame
✔ Optional: colored duct tape, stickers, string, decorative buttons, magnet strips

1 Make two double-sided strips that are each 3-3/4 inches long (see page 7).

2 Make two double-sided strips that are each 9-1/2 inches long.

3 Form the frame with the strips by placing the short pieces in between the long side pieces.

4 Cut four 1-inch long strips. Use them to tape the frame together where the long and short pieces meet.

5 Flip the frame over. Cut two strips of duct tape, each 9 inches long.

6 Place one strip directly over the short side of the frame, as shown. Fold extra tape onto the back.

7 Repeat Step 6 on the opposite short side.

8 Flip the frame over. Center the picture, face down, over the frame's window.

9 Cut two 9-inch strips. Use them to tape the picture onto the frame on the long sides.

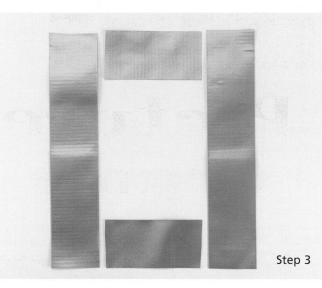

Step 3

Step 4

Step 7

Step 9

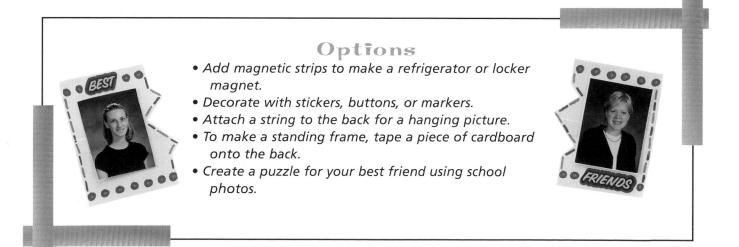

Options

- *Add magnetic strips to make a refrigerator or locker magnet.*
- *Decorate with stickers, buttons, or markers.*
- *Attach a string to the back for a hanging picture.*
- *To make a standing frame, tape a piece of cardboard onto the back.*
- *Create a puzzle for your best friend using school photos.*

Bowl

DIFFICULTY: ADVANCED

The bowl is a complicated project, because it is hard to imagine how the flat strips become round. I stumbled across it one time when I was just playing with tape. Who knows what you'll come up with!

You Will Need
✔ Duct tape
✔ Scissors
✔ Ruler
✔ Optional: colored duct tape, stickers, Sharpies, beaded fringe

1 Cut a 12-inch strip of tape. Lay it sticky side up on your work surface.

2 Cut another 12-inch strip. Place it sticky side up, in the center of the first strip, forming a cross.

3 Cut two more 12-inch strips. Place them sticky side up, diagonal to the first two strips.

4 Cut four 12-inch strips. Place one on each of the strips that are sticky side up.

5 Choose two neighboring strips to be "A" and "B."

6 Cut a piece of tape about 4 inches long. Place half of it sticky side down on strip A, as shown.

7 Now turn all of the strips over. Lift strips A and B toward you until their edges meet.

8 Press the remaining tape to strip B to hold it in place.

9 Repeat Steps 6 to 8 for the remaining strips until your bowl is complete.

10 Trim all of the way around the bowl so the top edge is even.

Step 4

Step 6

Step 8

Place Mat

Whether you make them for yourself, your pet, or for special family meals, duct tape place mats are very practical—they repel water and stains, clean up with a wipe, and can be decorated in any way.

You Will Need

✔ Duct tape
✔ Scissors
✔ Ruler or tape measure
✔ Optional: colored duct tape, stickers, paint markers

To make a place mat, just make a duct tape sheet (see page 6). Remember to trim off any sticky edges. Here are some suggested sizes:
Large: 16 inches long by seven strips
Medium: 14 inches long by six strips
Small: 12 inches long by five strips

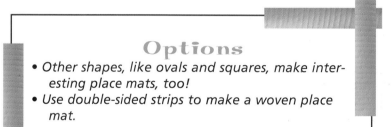

Options
• *Other shapes, like ovals and squares, make interesting place mats, too!*
• *Use double-sided strips to make a woven place mat.*

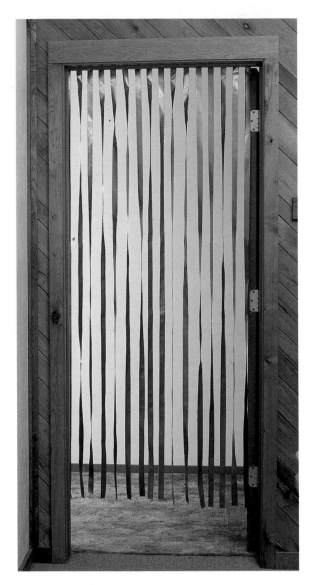

Door Streamers

DIFFICULTY: INTERMEDIATE

Need a little privacy even when your door is open? If so, this is the project for you!

You Will Need

- ✔ Duct tape
- ✔ Scissors
- ✔ Door frame
- ✔ Optional: colored duct tape, tacks or pins

1 Stick the end of the roll of duct tape to the top of the door frame

2 Roll out tape until the roll touches the floor (or other desired length); cut.

3 Starting at the bottom, carefully fold the strip in half, all of the way to the top.

4 Measure the width of the door.

5 Using the strip created in Step 3 as a guide, make as many strips as the width of the door.

6 Cut a strip equal to the width of the door; this will be the band that holds the streamers.

7 Lay the strip sticky side up on your work space.

8 Place long streamers so the top inch of each one is on the band. Place strips side by side, with or without space between them.

9 When all of the strips are placed, fold the band in half, sandwiching the strips.

10 Use pins, tacks, or tape to attach the streamers to the top of the door frame.

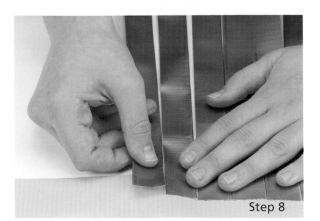

Step 8

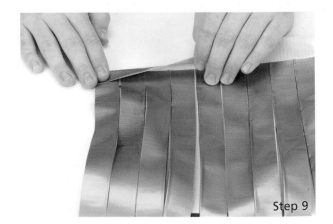

Step 9

Coasters

DIFFICULTY: VERY EASY

Made large enough, a coaster could double as a Frisbee!

You Will Need

✔ Duct tape

✔ Scissors

✔ Bowl or cup to trace

✔ Optional: colored duct tape, stickers, paint markers, Sharpies, yarn

1 Make a duct tape sheet that is 5 inches long by three strips wide (see page 6).

2 Use a cup or bowl to trace a circle onto the sheet; cut. Optional: You can also cut a square, star, or any other shape you want.

Mug

DIFFICULTY: ADVANCED

One time, a couple of my friends dared me to drink something out of a duct tape mug I'd made. I knew that the contents of duct tape—adhesive, string, and plastic—were nothing to be afraid of. So, I chugged down a mug full of water. It had a strange aftertaste, but a person could get used to it!

You Will Need

✔ Duct tape

✔ Scissors

✔ Bowl or cup to trace

✔ String

✔ Optional: colored duct tape, stickers, paint markers

Continued on the next page.

1 Make a duct tape sheet 5 inches long by three strips wide (see page 6).

2 Use a cup or bowl to trace a circle; cut out.

3 Use a string to measure the distance around the circle.

4 Make a duct tape sheet four strips wide by the length of the string in Step 3, plus 1 inch (to allow for trimming).

5 Cut an 8-inch strip of duct tape.

6 Bring the shorter edges of the duct tape sheet together to form a cylinder.

7 Use the 8-inch strip cut in Step 5 to tape the edges together, folding any extra over the top or bottom edge of the cylinder.

8 Cut a 3-inch piece of duct tape. Put half of the strip (the long way) on the bottom edge of the cylinder.

9 Cut slits in the remaining half of the strip every half inch to create tabs.

Step 2

Step 7

Step 3

Step 9

10 Place the circle cut in Step 2 in the bottom of the cylinder to form the bottom of the mug. Fold the tabs cut in Step 9 onto the circle, making a smooth edge.

11 Repeat Steps 8 to 10 until the entire bottom is attached to the cylinder.

12 To create the handle, make a folded strip that's 6 inches long (see page 7).

13 Cut two 2-inch strips. Use them to attach the handle to the mug. Don't forget to make a bulge in the handle so there is something to grip and your hand can fit through.

14 Cut two 6-inch strips to reinforce the handle. Tape them onto the mug on each side of the handle, covering the ends of the 2-inch strips in Step 13.

Step 10

Step 11

Step 13

Step 14

Options
• *Decorate the mug with photos and make it a "mug shot."*
• *If you've made your mug really well, it should hold water. Try it out!*

MUG SHOT

Chapter 4 Hold Everything!

T he first thing I ever saw made out of duct tape was a wallet. I thought it was so cool, and I wondered how anyone could have thought of it. Now that I've got more duct tape experience, I realize that wallets and other holders are just so practical! As time goes on, I am collecting more cards, CDs, and other miscellaneous items that need to be held. I hope these convenient projects help you hold it all together!

Purse

DIFFICULTY: ADVANCED

Purses are a challenge, because they require a pattern and are complicated to assemble—but it is worth the effort!

You Will Need

✔ Duct tape
✔ Scissors
✔ Ruler
✔ Optional: colored duct tape, stickers, fringe

1 Make a duct tape sheet that is 16 inches long by four strips wide (see page 6).

2 Use the pattern on page 30 to cut out the front, back, and bottom of the purse. **Note:** The pattern for the front and back is the same; cut two.

3 Lay the front piece on top of the back piece.

4 Cut two 6-1/2 inch strips. Use them to tape the long sides together.

5 Cut five 2-inch pieces of duct tape. Place them around the entire edge of the bottom piece so there are no spaces between the strips.

6 Make slits in the strips attached to the bottom every 1/2 inch. Cut the slits just to the edge of the bottom piece, all of the way around, to make tabs.

7 Lay the bottom piece on your work space, with the sticky side of the tabs up.

8 Squeeze the purse from the sides so the opening is shaped like the bottom piece. Guide it down onto the bottom piece.

9 Fold the tabs up onto the lower edge of the purse, making sure there are no gaps between the edge of the bottom piece and the lower edge of the purse.

10 Cut an 11-inch strip. Use it to make a band around the bottom of the purse, covering all of the tabs.

11 Make a folded strip as long as you want for the strap (see page 7).

12 Use two 2-inch pieces of tape to connect both ends of the strap to the inside of the purse.

13 Optional: Add a pocket on the inside or outside by making a duct tape sheet the size you want the pocket to be. Use strips to tape it on, leaving the upper edge open.

Options
- *Make a shorter strap for a handbag.*
- *If you feel ambitious, you could add a flap or a zipper; just tape them in place.*

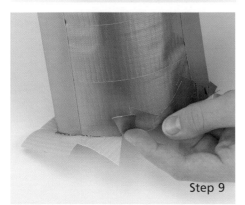

Step 4

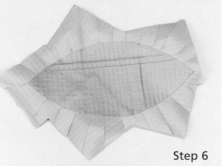

Step 6

Step 8

Step 9

Step 10

Step 12

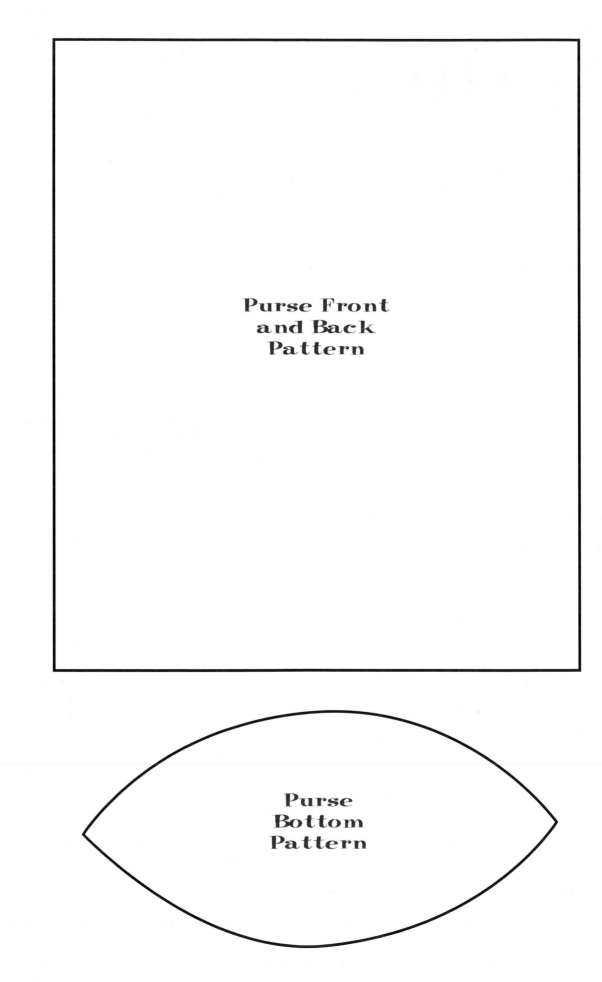

**Purse Front
and Back
Pattern**

**Purse
Bottom
Pattern**

Wallet

DIFFICULTY: EASY

When my friends turned 16, I made them wallets with a pocket for their driver's license!

You Will Need

✔ Duct tape
✔ Scissors
✔ Ruler
✔ Optional: colored duct tape, stickers, Sharpies, paint markers

1 Make a duct tape sheet that is 7 inches long by four strips wide (see page 6).

2 Fold the sheet in half so you have a rectangle.

3 Use a piece of tape about 4 inches long to seal the edge on one of the short sides of the rectangle. Trim off the extra tape.

4 Fold the wallet in half so the short sides line up. **Note:** Do this **before** taping the other side so that the wallet will fold without bulges.

5 Keep the wallet in the folded position and tape the other side. Trim excess.

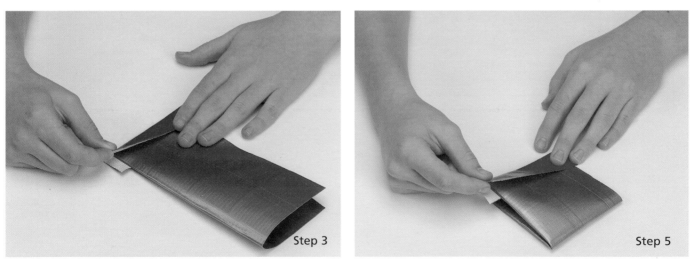

Step 3

Step 5

Options

• *Personalize your wallet with your initials, favorite colors, or your own personal trademark (my friend Bethany loves zebras...).*
• *You can include a pocket for your driver's license, credit cards, or gift certificates. See the purse (page 29, Step 13).*

Pocket Picture ID Holder

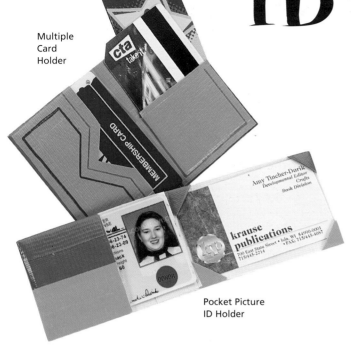

Multiple Card Holder

Pocket Picture ID Holder

Amy Tincher-Durik
Developmental Editor
Crafts
Book Division

krause
publications
700 East State Street • Iola, WI 54990-0001
715/445-2214 • FAX: 715/445-4067

DIFFICULTY: INTERMEDIATE

Are you always fumbling for your ID cards? Make it easy for yourself and everyone in line behind you with this holder!

You Will Need

✔ Duct tape
✔ Scissors
✔ Ruler
✔ Pencil
✔ Optional: colored duct tape, stickers

1 Make a duct tape sheet 10 inches long by two strips wide (see page 6). Trim the sheet to 9-1/2 inches by 2-3/8 inches.

2 Draw a line 2 inches from the short edge of the sheet. Fold on the line.

3 Cut two 1-inch strips. Use them to seal the side edges of the folded section and form a pocket.

4 Fold the holder in half, bringing the short edges together.

5 Cut a 1-inch strip of duct tape. Fold it in half to form a square. Make two diagonal cuts to create four triangular pieces.

6 Place the triangular pieces on the half without the pocket, two on the outer corners and two directly on the crease.

7 Cut a 1-inch strip of duct tape. Cut the strip in half the long way. Cut both strips in half again the short way.

8 Tape the triangles positioned in Step 6 in place with the strips, folding the edges onto the back side.

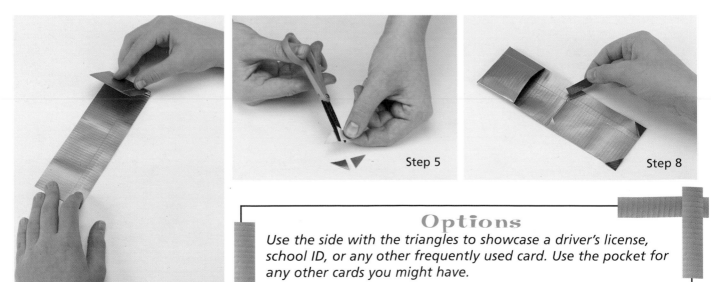

Step 5

Step 8

Step 3

Options

Use the side with the triangles to showcase a driver's license, school ID, or any other frequently used card. Use the pocket for any other cards you might have.

Multiple Card Holder

DIFFICULTY: INTERMEDIATE

Is you wallet overflowing with cards instead of money? Get organized with a multiple card holder!

You Will Need

✔ Duct tape
✔ Scissors
✔ Ruler
✔ Pencil
✔ Optional: colored duct tape, paint markers

1 Make a duct tape sheet that is 5 inches long by two strips wide (see page 6).

2 Fold the sheet in half, bringing the short sides together.

3 Make a 6-inch double-sided strip (see page 7).

4 Draw a line 2-1/4 inches from the short end of the strip. Cut on the line to form two pieces.

5 Cut a triangle in the center top edge of the larger piece. This will serve as a thumb grip and viewer for the cards.

6 Line up the corners of the larger piece with a short edge of the sheet from Step 2.

7 Cut two 1-inch strips of duct tape. Use the strips to attach the large piece to the sheet, as shown.

8 Cut a 4-inch strip. Use it to seal the bottom edge. Trim.

9 Place the small piece (cut in Step 4) 1/4 inch from the bottom of the other half of the holder.

10 Cut a 3-inch strip of duct tape. Place it over the small piece from Step 9 so that one edge starts at the fold, and the bottom edges line up to form a pocket for the cards. Fold extra tape onto the back of the holder.

Step 2

Step 5

Step 7

Step 8

Options
Make a viewing window out of clear tape to keep your most commonly used cards visible.

Step 10

Accordion-style CD Holder

DIFFICULTY: ADVANCED

Here's a new spin on CD holders! This project holds six CDs.

You Will Need
- ✔ Duct tape
- ✔ Scissors
- ✔ Ruler
- ✔ Optional: stickers, paint markers, Sharpies

1 Make a duct tape sheet that is 25 inches long by six strips wide (see page 6).

2 From the sheet, cut out ten squares that each measure 5 x 5 inches.

3 Use the CD pocket pattern on page 36 to cut a dip in six of the squares.

4 To make the front pocket of the CD holder, lay one dip-cut square over one plain square.

5 Cut three 5-inch pieces of duct tape to seal the two sides and bottom of the front pocket.

6 Repeat Steps 4 and 5 to make the back pocket.

7 To make an inside pocket, sandwich one plain square between two dip-cut squares.

8 Cut three pieces of 5-inch long duct tape to seal the two sides and bottom of the inside pocket.

9 Repeat Steps 7 and 8 to make a second inside pocket.

10 To assemble the CD holder, lay the front cover pocket dip side up to the left of an inside pocket. Use a 5-inch piece of tape to connect the two pockets.

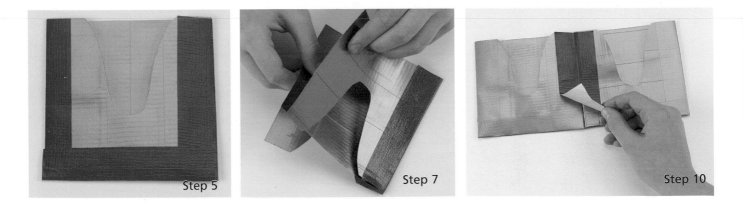

Step 5

Step 7

Step 10

11 Fold the front cover onto the inside pocket. Use another 5-inch piece of tape to reinforce the outside fold. Apply tape in the folded position.

12 Lay these two pockets flat with the side you just taped facing upward.

13 Place the second inside pocket next to the first. Connect with a 5-inch piece of duct tape.

14 Fold the second inside pocket onto the first inside pocket. Reinforce the outside fold with a 5-inch piece of tape while in the folded position.

15 Unfold all pockets. Place the holder in front of you so that the front cover pocket is dip side up.

16 Place the back cover pocket dip side up. Use a 5-inch piece of duct tape to connect it to the final inside pocket.

17 Fold the back cover pocket onto the inside pocket. Reinforce the outside fold with a 5-inch piece of duct tape while in the folded position.

18 Fold the pockets accordion-style, as shown.

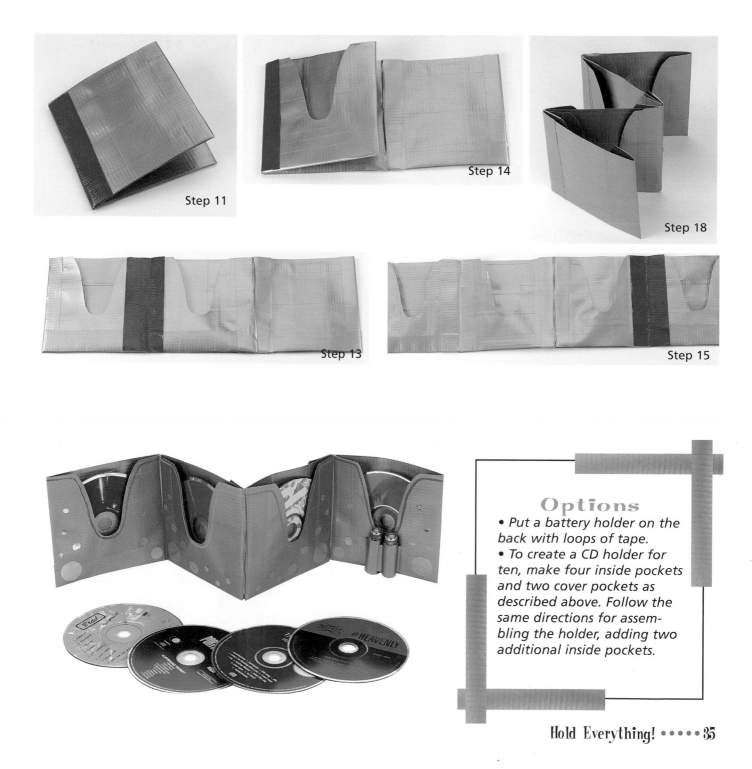

Step 11

Step 14

Step 18

Step 13

Step 15

Options
• Put a battery holder on the back with loops of tape.
• To create a CD holder for ten, make four inside pockets and two cover pockets as described above. Follow the same directions for assembling the holder, adding two additional inside pockets.

**CD
Pocket
Pattern**

Supply Box

DIFFICULTY: ADVANCED

I created this box to carry my duct tape supplies while working on this book.

You Will Need

✔ Duct tape
✔ Scissors
✔ Ruler
✔ Optional: colored duct tape, paint markers, Sharpies

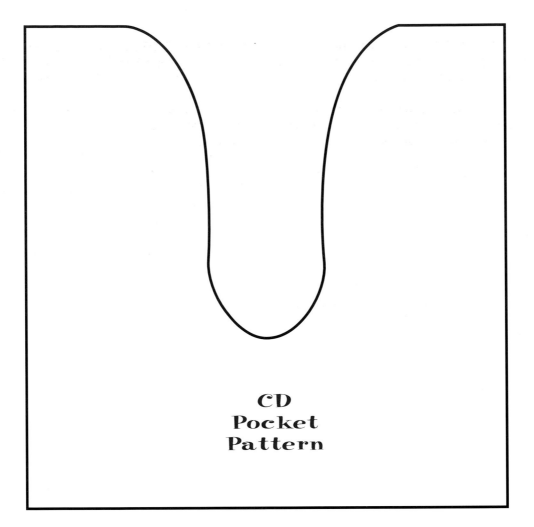

1 Make two duct tape sheets 6 inches long by four strips wide (see page 6). One will become the lid, and one will become the bottom, of the supply box.

2 Make two 6-inch double-sided strips and two 7-1/2-inch double-sided strips. (see page 7); these will become the sides of the supply box.

3 Place the strips along the four edges of the bottom sheet.

4 Cut two 6-inch strips and two 7-1/2-inch strips. Use them to tape the sides to the bottom of the supply box, as shown.

5 Flip the bottom and side panels over. Fold one short and one long side up. Use a 2-inch piece of duct tape to connect the sides on the outside corner, as shown.

6 Repeat Step 5 for the remaining three corners.

7 Make a 10-1/2-inch double-sided strip. Cut it so you have one 3-inch piece and one 7-1/2-inch piece; these will be the box dividers.

8 Attach dividers to the box with 2-inch strips, as shown, to make three compartments.

9 Cut a strip 7-1/2 inches long and use it to connect the lid to the box on the outside.

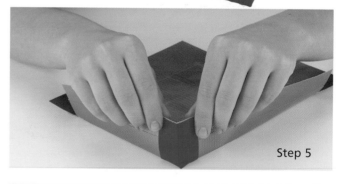

Step 4

Step 5

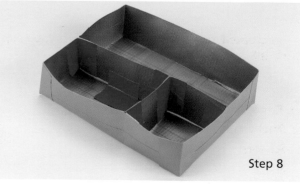

Step 8

Options

Use duct tape, or punch a hole in the lid and side and use a string, to keep the box shut.

Chapter 5 Fun and Games

A lot of the projects in this chapter are things I made just for fun. Most came about to amuse people when they were bored. My personal favorite is postcards because the possibilities are endless! You can impress your friends with your ability to get the ball in the cup, and become the King or Queen of Duct Tape in a crown or tiara.

Postcards

DIFFICULTY: VERY EASY

Postcards were some of the first things I ever made out of duct tape; previously, I had made postcards out of tin foil, cereal boxes, and bubble gum wrappers. I love sending and receiving mail, and I like finding new and creative ways to shock my friends!

You Will Need

✔ Duct tape

✔ Scissors

✔ Ruler

✔ Optional: colored duct tape, stickers, paint markers, Sharpies, jiggly eyes

3 Write your message on one side. Put the full address on the other side and use a first-class stamp. **Note:** Duct tape is heavier than a regular postcard, so it will not get delivered with only a postcard stamp.

1 Make a duct tape sheet 6 inches long by three strips wide (see page 6).

2 Optional: You can cut your sheet into a circle, square, or any other shape you like.

Tip

Be sure to write on the postcard with something that won't rub off (see page 5 for suggestions).

Hula Skirt

DIFFICULTY: INTERMEDIATE

Aloha! Welcome to duct tape paradise!

You Will Need

✔ Duct tape
✔ Scissors
✔ Tape measure
✔ Optional: colored duct tape

1 Measure from your waist to your knee (or to wherever you want the length of the skirt to be).

2 Cut a strip of duct tape to this length and make a folded strip (see page 7).

3 Take your waist measurement in inches. The number of inches will tell you how many strips to make; for example, a 28-inch waist means you should make twenty-eight strips to hang from the waistband. Make the strips as described in Step 2.

4 To make the waistband, cut a strip of duct tape to the waist measurement plus 3 inches.

5 Lay the waistband strip sticky side up on your work surface.

6 Place skirt strips so the top inch of each one is on the band. Place strips side by side without space between them.

7 When all strips are placed, fold the band in half, sandwiching the strips.

8 To wear the skirt, wrap it around your waist and tape it together where the waistband ends meet. Trim any overlapping tape.

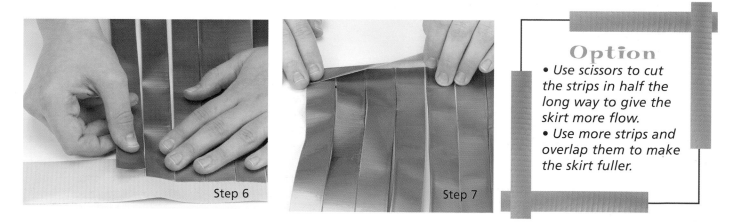

Step 6

Step 7

Option
• *Use scissors to cut the strips in half the long way to give the skirt more flow.*
• *Use more strips and overlap them to make the skirt fuller.*

Sandals

DIFFICULTY: EASY

It might be fun to have some sandals to wear with your hula skirt!

You Will Need

✔ Duct tape
✔ Scissors
✔ Shoe or sandal to trace
✔ Sharpie or pen
✔ Optional: colored duct tape, stickers, paint markers

Style 1

1 Make a duct tape sheet big enough so that you can trace around a pair of your shoes (see page 6).

2 Put both shoes on the sheet. Trace around them and cut out.

3 Make a sheet 8 inches long by three strips wide. Cut in half the long way; these will be the straps.

4 Attach the strap to the bottom of the sandal with duct tape.

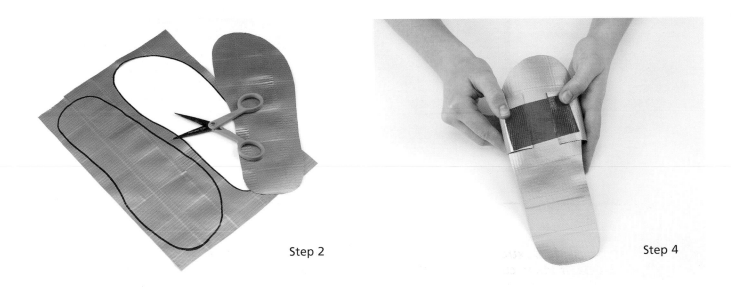

Step 2

Step 4

Style 2

1 Repeat Steps 1 and 2 in Sandals, Style 1 directions, on the opposite page.

2 Put your feet on the sandals and use a pen to make a mark in between your big toe and the toe next to it.

3 Make a fold 'n' roll strip 10 inches long (see page 8) and cut it in half to make two 5-inch strips.

4 Cut two 1-inch pieces of tape. Use them to tape one end of one 5-inch strip onto the mark and the other end to the bottom of the sandal.

5 Repeat Step 4 for the other strip, taping one end on top of the first strap.

6 Repeat Steps 3 to 5 for the remaining sandal.

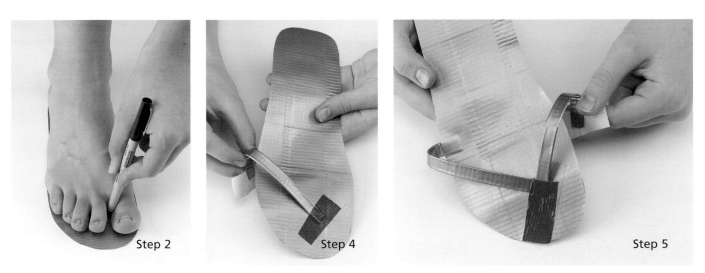

Step 2   Step 4   Step 5

Options

You can add extra layers of duct tape to the bottom of the sandals, or cut some layers of foam, cushion, or cardboard using the sandal as a pattern. Attach them with strips of duct tape. This will make your sandals much more comfortable if you want to wear them.

Crown and Tiara

DIFFICULTY: CROWN VERY EASY/TIARA EASY

For my grandparents' fiftieth anniversary, I made them a duct tape crown and tiara. They were the King and Queen for the day! Any birthday party or family celebration can benefit from a duct tape crown.

You Will Need

✔ Duct tape

✔ Scissors

✔ Tape measure or string

✔ Optional: colored duct tape, stickers, plastic rhinestones (attach with hot glue gun; for adult, or supervised, use only!)

Crown

1 Use a piece of string or a tape measure to measure your head.

2 Make a duct tape sheet that is the measurement long by three strips wide (see page 6).

3 Trim off sticky edges.

4 Cut triangles on one long edge to form a basic crown.

5 Use a 2-inch piece of tape to join the two loose ends together to form a ring.

Step 4

Tiara

1 Make a duct tape sheet that is 10 inches long by two strips wide (see page 6).

2 Use the pattern or make up your own design to cut out the top piece of the tiara.

3 Measure your head with a string or tape measure. Cut a piece of duct tape this length.

4 Lay the strip sticky side up on your work surface.

5 Center the top piece of the tiara on the strip, as shown.

6 Fold the bottom half of the band up, sandwiching the top piece of the tiara.

7 Use a 2-inch piece of duct tape to join the two loose ends of the band together to form a ring.

Tiara Pattern

Bowl instructions can be found on page 22.

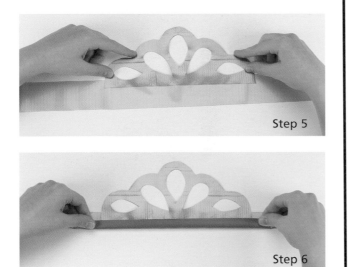

Step 5

Step 6

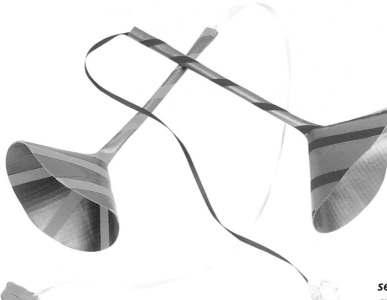

Cup 'n' Ball Game

One time when I visited my Uncle Greg, it seemed like he needed a challenge. I made this game for him with a piece of string and the duct tape I always have with me.

You Will Need

✔ Duct tape
✔ Scissors
✔ Bowl or cup to trace
✔ Ruler
✔ String or ribbon
✔ Pencil
✔ Optional: colored duct tape, paint markers

Cup

1 Make a duct tape sheet that is 4 inches long by two strips wide (see page 6).

2 Use a cup or bowl to trace a circle. Cut out the circle.

3 Draw a dot in the middle of the circle. Make a straight cut from the edge of the circle to the dot.

4 Make another straight cut from the edge so the piece removed is one-quarter of the circle.

5 Cut a strip of duct tape about 1/2 inch long.

6 Bring the edges of the circle together and use the strip to tape the seam and make a cone.

7 Snip 1/4 inch off the tip of the cone; this is where the handle will be attached.

Handle

8 Make a 6-inch fold 'n' roll strip (see page 8).

9 Cut another 6-inch strip of duct tape. Lay it sticky side up on your work surface.

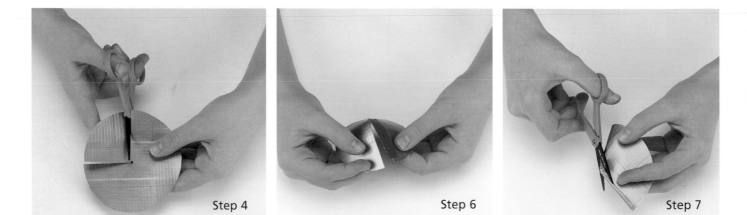

Step 4   Step 6   Step 7

10 Cut a 12-inch piece of string or ribbon. Stick 1/2 inch of the ribbon on the bottom right corner of the strip, as shown.

11 Place the fold 'n' roll strip from Step 8 on the bottom edge of the second strip, covering the ribbon.

12 Use the fold 'n' roll technique again until you have a double-layered handle with a string coming out of one end.

13 Stick 1/4 inch of the handle into the snipped end of the cone, as shown.

14 Cut a small strip of tape about 1/2 inch long. Cut it again the short way so you have two pieces. Use one small strip on each side of the handle to connect it to the cone.

Ball

15 Cut a 6-inch piece of duct tape. Put 1/2 inch of the ribbon onto the duct tape. Crumple and roll the duct tape into a ball around the ribbon.

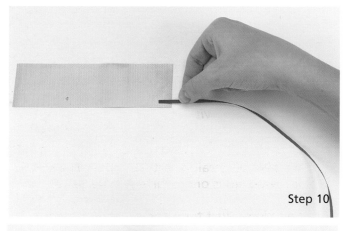

Step 10

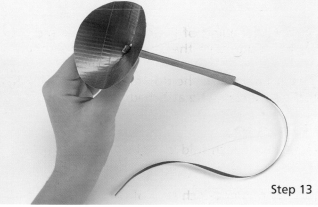

Step 13

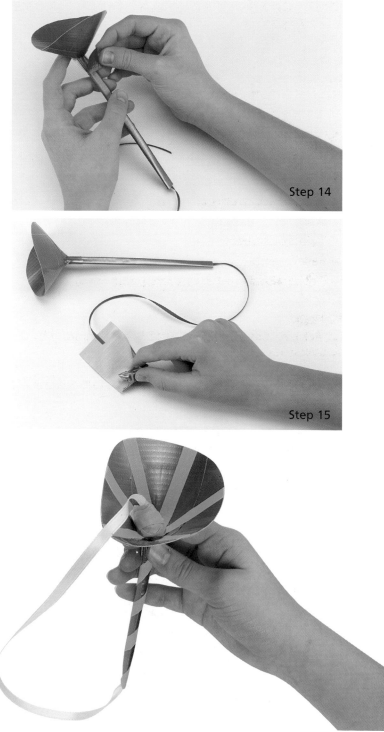

Step 14

Step 15

Options

To make the game harder, you can make the string longer, or make the cone smaller by cutting the circle in half instead of taking out one quarter in Step 4.

Transportable Basketball Game

When I was younger, I always wanted one of those basketball hoops you hang on the back of the door, but I never got one. So I made my own! This is a game you can play anywhere.

You Will Need

✔ Duct tape

✔ Scissors

✔ Ruler

✔ Scotch tape or tacks

✔ Optional: colored duct tape, paint markers, stickers

1 Cut a strip of duct tape 10 inches long. Make a folded strip (see page 7).

2 Take a small piece of tape and tape the ends together to form a ring.

3 To make the backboard, make a duct tape sheet that is 6 inches long by three strips wide (see page 6).

4 Use a small piece of tape to attach the ring to the backboard.

5 Attach the backboard to a wall, door, or other surface you want to play on with Scotch tape or tacks.

6 To make a basketball, take a 12- to 14-inch strip of tape and ball it up, or roll up duct tape scraps and cover with a layer of fresh tape.

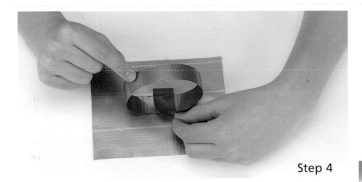

Step 4

Options

Make a bowl (page 22) and attach it to the backboard instead of a hoop. Besides having it catch your basketballs, it can also store them when you're not playing.

Checkerboard

DIFFICULTY: INTERMEDIATE

A few years ago, we were visiting our relatives in Montana, and there were a lot of second cousins. One day the weather was bad and they couldn't play outside, so I made a checkerboard for them to play with. You can use just about anything for the pieces, including candy or duct tape circles!

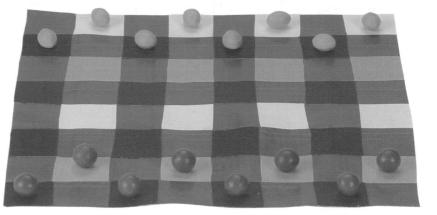

You Will Need

✔ Duct tape, gray and colored
✔ Scissors
✔ Ruler

1 Make a sheet that is 9 inches long by five strips wide (see page 6).

2 Trim the sheet to a perfect 8- by 8-inch square.

3 Cut an 8-inch strip of a contrasting color of duct tape.

4 Cut this strip in half the long way.

5 Use your ruler to cut each strip into 1-inch squares.

Row 1

6 Place the first square on the top left-hand corner, lining up the edges of the small square with the edges of the big square.

7 Place the second square 1 inch away from the first square, lining up the top edges.

8 Continue this way until you have four squares and four spaces in the top row.

Row 2

9 For the second row, start with a 1-inch space, and then place a 1-inch square of tape (can be another contrasting color). The bottom corners of squares in Row 1 should touch the top corners of squares in Row 2.

Remaining Rows

10 Continue to place 1-inch squares on the board, alternating as in Steps 6 to 8.

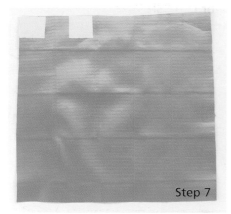

Step 7

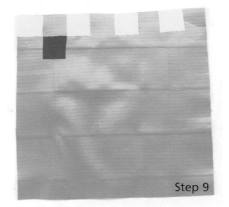

Step 9

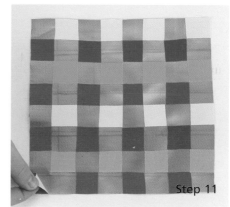

Step 11

Scrap Ball

Instead of throwing your duct tape scraps away, save them and make a duct tape ball. I saved my scraps for three months while I was working on this book and made this large scrap ball! Just push all of your scraps together and cover with a fresh layer of tape to make your very own!

Resources

Duct Tape

Projects featured in this book are made with Duck brand duct tape, manufactured by Manco, Inc. Visit Manco's websites for lots of interesting facts about duct tape and to find out about its kids club. www.manco.com and www.ducktapeclub.com

Scissors

The scissors shown throughout this book are Fiskars non-stick scissors. www.fiskars.com

Stickers

Stickers used to embellish the projects in this book are from:
Frances Meyer, Inc. www.francesmeyer.com
Mrs. Grossman's. www.mrsgrossmans.com

NRN Designs. www.nrndesigns.com
Provocraft. www.provocraft.com
Reynolds. www.reynoldscrafts.com
Sandylion. www.sandylion.com
Stickopotamus. www.stickopotamus.com

Markers and Pens

The permanent paint markers and pens used in this book are:
Painty brand by EKSuccess. www.eksuccess.com
DECOCOLOR by Marvy. www.marvy.com
Sharpies by Sanford. www.sanfordcorp.com

Buttons

Buttons used to decorate projects shown in this book are by JHB Int'l. www.buttons.com